Epic Sports Stories For Young Achievers

Inspire Your Child to Greatness Through the Amazing Journeys of Legendary Athletes

Hayden Fox

1

Claim your free gifts!

(My way of saying thank you for your support)

Simply visit **haydenfoxmedia.com** to receive the following:

- 10 Powerful Dinner Conversations To Create Amazing Kids

- 10 Magical Affirmations To Help Kids Become Unstoppable in Life

(you can also scan this QR code)

4

This book belongs to

_____

Table of Contents

Introduction

Hey, young achiever! Are you ready to be inspired to achieve greatness? Are you ready to learn how famous athletes conquered their sports? If your answer is yes, then get ready to be amazed by the legendary stories of some of the most incredible athletes of all time!

These athletes have seen it all—pain, sorrow, disappointment, you name it. But they never gave up. They fought their battles and carved out paths of their own. While you may know these athletes' successes from television, magazines, and other media, you may not be aware of the stories behind those successes. Those stories are precisely what bring us here.

This book explores the inspiring journeys of famous athletes, from their humble beginnings to becoming the best in their sports.

Every athlete in this book has faced unique struggles and has a distinct story to share. Yet, what they all share is an incredible ability to overcome adversity and leave a lasting impact on the world of sports.

Their life experiences led to both success and a beautiful journey. These athletes kept going amid hunger, amid bullying, and even when the pain seemed way too much. They exemplify what it means to be courageous, ambitious, and resilient, and they show that no setback is enough to keep you from chasing your dreams.

From podiums to arenas to stadiums and courts, we will meet these stars and get a feel for what it really takes to succeed.

The stories in this book will elevate your mood when things aren't looking too good. They will be a comfort zone and a reference for all of life's lessons. They'll give you the push you need to get up and go for your dreams, to overcome your challenges and create the life you have imagined.

So, prepare to embark on a journey that could change how you view life and set the stage for your pursuit of legendary successes.

To kick things off, let's travel back in time to the early chapters in the story of the legendary Babe Ruth.

Please note: *The quotes included in this book are creative additions intended to enhance the stories while maintaining the general theme of the events.*

Babe Ruth

*I like to give my best; I either do it big or fail
dismally. I like to live a life of grandeur.*

Many people have played baseball, but only a few have left behind a lasting legacy on the scale of Babe Ruth's. Through the 1920s and '30s, Babe amazed audiences with his extraordinary athletic abilities, establishing himself as a force to be reckoned with. Even people unfamiliar with baseball knew his name. Babe Ruth elevated the popularity of baseball during a time when it wasn't widely followed. Though he is no longer with us, his name continues to hold continued significance in history. With his larger-than-life persona, he embodied the essence of American sports, and he remains an iconic figure in sports till this day.

However, Ruth's journey was not without its challenges. His life was filled with triumphs and setbacks, moments of joy and times of sorrow. To truly grasp what it meant to be Babe Ruth, we must go back to 1895 when it all began. So, prepare yourself for an adventure as we step into our time machine and travel back to the 1800s!

Childhood and Early Life of Babe Ruth

The man who was later known as Babe Ruth was born George Herman Ruth Jr. on February 6, 1895, as the first child of Kate Shamberger Ruth and George Herman Ruth Sr. Having been born into a rough neighborhood of Baltimore, Maryland, George came from the humblest of beginnings.

Growing up in Baltimore was challenging. Out of eight children born in his family, only he and his younger sister, Mamie, lived past infancy and into adulthood. Adding to the complications of his upbringing, his father was a saloon owner and an alcoholic who often recklessly indulged in the beer intended for his business. Meanwhile, his mother was sickly, leaving her very little time to take care of her kids. His parents' circumstances led to the rumor that young George was an orphan.

This lack of parental attention led him astray and out on the streets of Baltimore, looking to fill the void in his heart. With this came nothing but trouble. George's lifestyle was riddled with petty theft and mischief on the rough, dusty streets. Not only that, but he also didn't go to school very often. Eventually, his parents grew tired of this behavior.

"I've had it with this boy, Kate. I've had it," his father huffed one night after George had been escorted home by a police officer.

"Tomorrow, first thing in the morning, I'm calling St. Mary's to see if they have got a space for him there!" he added.

"Oh, George, that's a bit harsh, don't you think? Give the boy a chance," his mother said as she tried to save her son.

"My mind's made up, Kate. Off the boy goes!" he concluded, before retiring to bed.

Just as he promised, George's father called the school the next day, and they were more than happy to say that indeed there was space for one more.

"Get ready, kid. The bus is coming to get ya in 30," his father shouted before slamming the door and going off to the saloon.

Hesitantly, George packed his suitcase and said his goodbyes to his mother and sister. At the age of just 7, he found himself at St. Mary's Industrial School for Boys, a school for incorrigibles (someone who cannot be reformed) and orphaned kids. George would stay there for the next 12 years of his life.

As he walked into the building, he instantly felt like the school was more of a prison. Thick walls with strips of paint peeling off them enclosed him, and he couldn't help but feel betrayed. Upon reaching the front counter, the first person he saw was a tall, tan gentleman with glasses who was dressed in a white robe. The man went by the name of Brother Matthias.

Brother Matthias was not just the school's discipline officer, but also a father figure for George, helping him change his unruly behavior.

"George, I have heard all about you. Loosen up, you are in good hands. This is your new home now," Brother Matthias told him. Undoubtedly the most painful thing that came with his enrollment at St. Mary's was that his family cut all ties with him, handing over full custody to the school.

That first day was one of the worst in George's life. Being surrounded by a completely new set of faces was hard to adjust to. However, the next day had something else in store for him.

That morning, Brother Matthias woke him up early and took him down a corridor and out onto a large green field—probably the best thing he had seen since his arrival at the school. Here, he had his very first encounter with baseball.

"Ever heard of baseball, George?" asked Brother Matthias.

George, who had never heard of the game, responded, "B-baseball? You mean a ball?"

Brother Matthias chuckled. "Not quite, although yes, it does involve a ball. Ya wanna take another guess, boy?"

"I'm afraid I'm out of guesses, Brother," George said with a sparkle in his eyes.

"Oh boy, you got a lot to learn, huh? But worry not, you'll be a pro in no time!" Brother Matthias grabbed a ball and bat and showed George how the sport is played.

The two spent the day playing the sport, with George gradually getting the hang of it. One day of practice turned into days, and George fell in love with baseball. Having found solace from his heartbreak, he was determined to use baseball as a vehicle to turn his life around. Every morning, George was up by 4 a.m. working on his pitching, footwork, and overall fitness for six hours each day. He knew it was all or nothing, and that he needed to chase his dream of being a successful baseball player with all his might.

"Life has something great in store for you, you just have to put in the work," he constantly reminded himself during his practices.

George's training paid off and at 16 years old, he became the school's most valuable baseball player, even though most players were older than him.

George remained consistent, adhering to his practice schedule and playing baseball as much as he could. He put his heart and soul into the game, often arriving first to practice.

By the time he was 19 years old, his pitching skills landed him an opportunity that marked the start of greater things to follow. One cold winter morning, George was out practicing like he did each morning, but this time he was joined by a buddy who hit while George pitched. Then an unfamiliar voice interrupted their game.

"You are darn good, boy," the voice said. George turned and found Jack Dunn, the coach of the Baltimore Orioles, a minor league team in Baltimore. "Would you like to become a part of my team?"

It all felt like a dream and George couldn't believe what was happening. "Me? Play for a real team? Are you serious?"

"Dead serious, kid! I'm impressed with what you got going on there. In fact, this is the kind of talent we are looking for," Dunn responded warmly.

George replied to Dunn's request with an ecstatic yes, and right there and then a contract for $600 dollars a year was signed in his name (Babe Ruth Biography, 2018). To seal the deal, St. Mary's also granted Dunn full custody over George, which meant that he was now George's full-time guardian.

Now the newest member of the Baltimore Orioles and no longer within the confines of St. Mary's, George was eager to meet the world. Everything seemed to amuse him, and at times he acted like a big baby. That, along with looking a lot younger than his age, caused his teammates to nickname him "Babe."

"Hey guys, there goes Jack Dunn's new babe," shouted his new teammates.

Babe only played with the Orioles for half a season, but his performance during that time was worth a lifetime. A left-handed pitcher, he won an astounding 14 games with the team, earning acclaim as a baseball player and becoming a people's favorite. Even people who weren't fans of baseball watched the sport just so they could see his incredible talent.

"Babe Ruth, Babe Ruth, Babe Ruth!" people chanted every time he walked by.

However, as they say, all good things come to an end. Jack Dunn faced bankruptcy, and the only way to recover from it was to sell one of his star players—none other than Babe Ruth.

Babe was sold to the Boston Red Sox, where he got his first opportunity to rub shoulders with the big leagues. At the Red Sox, Babe continued to amaze the crowds with each game he played.

He became so good that between 1915 and 1919, he won an impressive number of accolades that only a few could match. During those five years, the pitcher showcased his aptitude for baseball, boasting 87 wins, including three World Series victories.

Reaching the Top

Babe's success was because of his unrelenting hard work and determination to become nothing but the best. The formula to his success was goal setting. Babe constantly set goals for the number of wins he wanted to achieve and focused his efforts on accomplishing those goals.

As if this were not enough, in 1919, when home runs were a rare occurrence, Babe hit a record 29. This exceeded the previous record of 27 set by Ned Williamson of the Chicago White Stockings.

In that year, Jacob Rupert from the New York Yankees heard about Babe Ruth's impressive offensive performances and made a generous offer to buy him.

"Come on, let me have the boy. I'll give you an arm and leg for him," Rupert begged as he negotiated with Ed Barrow, who managed the Red Sox then.

"I don't know, man. I really like the boy," a reluctant Barrow responded.

Rupert bargained, "Alright, I'll give you $125,000!"

"Deal!" Barrow said.

Rupert didn't have to give up his limbs, and in 1920, Babe made the move to New York.

The trade proved to be a colossal blunder for the Red Sox. After parting ways with Babe, they didn't win another World Series until 2004. They called the drought The Curse of the Bambino, citing the historic moment in Red Sox history.

However, from the moment Babe went to New York, he became one with the Yankees.

The team's fortunes aligned with the signing of Babe as they soon went on to win their very first title.

Because both pitching and hitting are complicated skills, most baseball players of Babe's time were either good pitchers or good hitters. Only a remote few were good at both. However, this is something Babe defied. Babe Ruth proved to be excellent at both, becoming the rare case of a well-rounded baseball player.

Now playing in the outfield, Babe instantly ascended to the top as one of the best hitters who ever played. To top that, he dominated scoreboards with a new record of 54 home runs in 1920, largely exceeding the runner-up who had 19.

At this point in his career, Babe was a one-of-kind player who revolutionized the way baseball was played. Many players adopted his playing style, which focused on home runs more than any other types of hits.

For Babe, it was go big or go home, and his fans loved it. The public love was evident in the influx of people into the Yankees' stadium whenever they played. As a result, in 1923 they had to move to a bigger stadium, the original Yankee Stadium, which became famously known as "The House That Ruth Built." Babe Ruth's unmatched credentials on the field led to a team regarded by many as the most prominent of all time. He left a permanent mark on the game.

Babe Ruth had it tough growing up. He had to overcome the disappointment of having his family disown him and dumping him in a school away from home. But most of all, he had to challenge himself, change his behavior, and transform his life. Babe was strong and was a true testament of the growth mindset at its best—he took his downfalls as opportunities to grow. He showed that throwing in the towel was not an option, and that is why we look up to him and respect him even to this day.

Post-Reading Reflection

Are you inspired to change your life just like Babe did? Do you want to become the best version of yourself and realize your goals? You can start here.

The Goal Pie

You can do this activity on your own, or with your parents or a friend. You will need a piece of paper and colored pencils.

Think of two of your biggest goals. These can be both long-term and short-term. Once you have established those, draw a large circle on the paper and divide it into two parts.

In each section, write the goal and how you want to achieve it. Add ideas until you have covered both sections, or pieces of the pie.

For example:

Goal: I want to get 90% in math this year.
How I will do this: - Attend extra classes, - watch online math videos, - do all my homework, and - study hard

Now that you know what steps you can take, you can start moving toward your goal.

Moving on to our next athlete, put on your best tennis outfit as we go to the courts to meet another sporting great, Maria Sharapova. Off we go!

Maria Sharapova

I'm not the next anyone, I'm the first Maria Sharapova.

Maria Sharapova, also known as "The Screaming Cinderella," is a five-time tennis Grand Slam winner and the only Russian woman to achieve this feat. Despite having received U.S. citizenship, she has shown her unwavering loyalty to her homeland, Russia. We can all learn from and apply that loyalty to our lives. Maria, who won numerous accolades and broke many records, is living proof that hard work, coupled with passion and talent, is indeed the recipe for success. However, beneath all the glistening triumph lies a story seldom told—Maria's challenging journey to stardom. So, without further ado, let's jump straight to the year 1987, when the legacy began. Lettt's gooooo!

Childhood and Early Life of Maria Sharapova

It was April 19, 1987, and the world had no idea what was coming its way. Not only a new child, but a prospective star was born to take over the world of tennis. Born Maria Yuryevna

Sharapova to her parents, Yuri and Yelena Sharapova, Maria enjoyed tennis early in her life alongside her close-knit family. She had tennis blood in her veins because her parents also loved the sport (Teqipadmin, 2023). Legend has it that Maria was only 4 years old when she grew fond of tennis. Maria's journey started with a makeshift tennis racket made of a chopped broomstick and a plastic lid.

"Mom, Dad! Look at me, I'm a superstar," Maria would assert every time she attempted to mimic her favorite tennis players.

Playing at almost any chance possible, she was determined to see herself on TV one day, competing at prestigious events. Luckily for her, the opportunity that would catapult her to her first step in that journey was just around the corner.

Maria's dad usually accompanied her to the local tennis clinic, where she would kill time playing for a greater part of the day. While at the clinic one day, a famous Czech-born tennis star, Martina Navratilova, spotted the young talent during her own training session. She was impressed by what she saw.

"That girl is a future professional!" Martina said as she dropped her racket and approached Maria and her father.

"What! Did you just hear that, Maria? The famous Martina Navratilova is convinced you are a star," her father said in awe.

Martina recommended sending Maria to Nick Bollettieri's Tennis Academy in Bradenton, Florida. "It's the only place this kind of excellence should go," Martina concluded before picking up her racket and continuing with her game.

An eager Maria and her father took the news home to inform her mother, who instantly gave her approval of the idea.

Having made up their minds, the family started preparing for their journey to the United States. However, a few roadblocks sprouted along the way. First, they did not have enough money, and second, Maria's mother was not eligible for an American visa. They asked their extended family for money so they could sustain their new lives in the U.S.. Although this mission was successful, they sadly had to part ways with Yelena.

"It's alright, go on without me. It's your time to shine. Till next time, my loves," her teary-eyed mother said at the airport before Maria and her father, Yuri, departed.

With only $700 and no knowledge of the English language, the pair landed in Florida (Teqipadmin, 2023). They did not waste any time and just a few days after their arrival in 1994, they made their way to Nick Bottilieri's Academy. To their disappointment, Maria was rejected because she was only 7 years old, a year below the minimum registration age of 8 years.

In addition to this low blow, they battled to keep up with the demands of their new life in America. Maria's father had to work many jobs in order to raise Maria's academy fees, to buy food, and to pay rent for the apartment they shared with an elderly Russian woman.

Although staying at the apartment was definitely better than being on the streets, the living conditions weren't exactly what one would call comfortable. The apartment was dilapidated and cramped, and the only place Maria and her father could sleep was a torn-up couch.

While her father was at work, Maria would capitalize on the time she had at her disposal. She dedicated her mornings to tennis practice and the rest of her day to self-study English in front of the television.

Finally, after a year, she was old enough to join Bollettieri's academy. Her father decided they should return to the school to see if Maria stood a chance.

Upon arriving at the academy, Maria showcased her talent, and she nailed it! Her lightning speed footwork and energy on the court left her audience excited.

"Bring me a scholarship contract and my favorite pen. The girl is a great fit for our academy!" exclaimed one of the directors.

Because of her prowess at the sport, the 8-year-old was exempted from paying the $46,000 yearly fee and instead enrolled on a fully paid scholarship. After a long wait, everything was falling into place. Maria was so close to achieving her dream of becoming a tennis player.

Although she was excited to finally get the expertise she needed, she faced an awful lot of obstacles at the academy. Her young age and deep Russian accent often made her the subject of bullying and ridicule. The other kids would tease her and connive to leave her out of their group activities.

"Get off the courts and go back to Russia!" one would shout from afar during practice sessions.

"Maybe you should just go play under a bus, you clueless little pest," another would holler.

After hearing these heavy insults, she would often cry and think: *What have I done to deserve this? If I am so horrible and can't fit in, then I'm probably a terrible tennis player. They are right. Maybe I should just go back home.*

Almost all days at the academy were painful to endure, and these thoughts constantly haunted her. However, her determination to succeed kept her going. She used tennis as an escape from all the mean kids. Every time she felt terrible, she would take her frustrations out on the tennis courts.

"Come on, Maria, you are better than this, I believe in you," she would motivate herself.

With these words of affirmation, all her problems and pains would disappear. Maria got into the habit of saying words of affirmation every morning before she went for another six hours on the tennis courts.

The words of the bullies no longer meant anything to her, and it was like everything they said just bounced off her without causing even the slightest harm. But the older girls persisted with their challenging behavior.

"I already told you to never come back here," said one of the girls, pushing Maria aside.

"You might need to get comfortable repeating that a couple more times because I will keep coming back," Maria said with a smirk on her face.

"If you think you are so good, then prove it," a girl told her one day.

Maria's heart skipped a beat. The other girls paused their games and watched eagerly as the two girls got ready to battle it out. A slight tinge of hatred showed on both their faces. The other girls were waiting for Maria to back out, but she did not give them any satisfaction.

Maria rose to the challenge, picked her racket up, looked her opponent in the eye, and said, "It's crunch time!"

Maria got straight to the game. She knew the odds were against her, but she gave all she could. For the first time in her life, she felt all the parts of her body in sync with one another. Maria showcased her talent as she anticipated and reciprocated her opponent's shots with ease.

On the other side of the net, her opponent's face turned red as she struggled to keep up with Maria's almost perfect performance. Finally— after going neck and neck for what felt like decades—Maria sent the winning ball flying, and it was game over for the opposition.

The other girls, now with a change of heart, cheered, "Maria, Maria, Maria!"

Maria couldn't have hoped for things to go any better. She defeated the big bully, not by hitting her or using mean words, but purely by using her talent. For this reason, she gained a newfound reputation at the academy. From that day onward, the girls who had previously dissed her all wished to befriend her.

The earliest bird catches the worm was her motto back at the academy. She would often be the first to arrive and the last to leave practice. Maria gave the game her all and was dedicated to improving her skill, aiming to be better than the previous day. Because of her talent, commitment, and hard work, she became an unstoppable force who stood out as one of the best products of the academy.

Reaching the Top

In 2000, at the age of just 13, four years after joining the academy, she took her career to a whole new level and went professional (Teqipadmin, 2023). That same year, she won her first of many competitions, winning the Eddie Herr International Junior Tennis Championship. She also earned the Rising Star Award, only bestowed upon extremely talented players.

Maria holds a spot as one of the most skilled female tennis players of all time, and her long list of achievements backs this up. Her career boasts five Grand Slam singles titles, meaning wins at tennis' biggest competitions. Maria won Wimbledon in 2004, the U.S. Open in 2006, the Australian Open in 2008, and the French Open in 2012 and 2014. The year 2005 marked the biggest highlight of her career, as she rose to the number 1 spot in the world rankings, a position she held for a good 21 weeks. The list goes on. Maria achieved an impressive record of 36 singles titles and five doubles titles on the Women's Tennis Association tour, in addition to winning a silver medal at the 2012 Olympic Games in London.

Maria never would have gone that far had she not been resilient and practiced. She didn't give up and throw herself a pity party. Instead, she cried and when she was done, she wiped her tears, got off her butt, and challenged herself! Even amid negativity and hate, she still had it in her to believe in herself. She worked hard, dedicating almost six hours daily to improving her skills, and above all, she trusted the process. In 2023, Maria was a multimillionaire business owner who is still striving to succeed.

Post-Reading Activities

Maria Sharapova was a powerhouse, not only in tennis but also in life. Below are some takeaways from her character. As you read, consider areas where you show your own power.

Emotional Intelligence

You can't control what people say about you and what they think about you.

You can't plan for bad luck.

You can only work your hardest and do your best and tell the truth.

In the end, it's the effort that matters. The rest is beyond your control. —Maria Sharapova

Maria knew how to deal with emotionally challenging situations and rise above adversity. Each time someone tried to bring her down, she motivated herself using positive affirmations. Use the prompts below to create your own positive affirmations that you can tell yourself when you are feeling down or doubting yourself.

Write these down in a journal or diary.

Here's an example of an affirmation to help you get started.

I am who I am, and that makes me special.

Now create your own affirmations using these sentence starters:

- I am good at:

- Today will be a great day because:

- Today, I will push myself harder to become:

- Because the sky's the limit, I can and will become:

With this chapter completed, it's time to jump right into the next one and explore the story of Cristiano Ronaldo's rise to international fame from humble beginnings.

Cristiano Ronaldo

I view myself as the top football player on the planet. Unless one has faith that they are the best, they will never make the most of their potential.

Some know him as CR7, others know him as Cristiano Ronaldo, but the fact of the matter is that either name equates to an unparalleled legacy! We all know him as a superstar, megastar, and legend, but very few know of the road that led to Cristiano Ronaldo's success. Born on the small island of Madeira southwest of Portugal in the Atlantic Ocean, life was far from easy. But if the saying "one's strength is measured by their ability to get up from the dirt and dust themselves off" is anything to go by, then he really did become one powerful person. Sickness, poverty, family issues—you name it, he overcame it. Let's explore the events that formed CR7.

Childhood and Early Life In Madeira

Cristiano Ronaldo was born on February 5, 1985, on the volcanic island of Madeira. However, his birth wasn't all that appreciated. When she found out she was pregnant, his mother was afraid she couldn't afford to support him, so she requested an abortion from doctors. The doctors refused to proceed with her request (Hendrix, 2016).

Ronaldo's birth was written in the stars, and nothing could have been done to stop it. Simply put, Ronaldo was born to become a soccer legend.

Growing up in Madeira, Cristiano had a tough start to his life. Although he had his three older siblings, Katia, Elma, and Hugo and his parents, Maria and Jose, by his side, the family often struggled to put food on the table.

Jose Ronaldo worked as a soldier and battled in the war against Mozambique and Angola. One day, he arrived at work only to be told that there no longer was a space for him. Disgruntled and demoralized by this misfortune, he instantly turned to alcohol for comfort.

His habits were not cheap, and they sometimes came at the expense of his family's well-being. Jose would spend all their money on alcohol instead of paying bills and buying food, which made their financial situation even worse.

Although Jose was always present for Ronaldo, his alcoholism stood in the way of the two ever getting an opportunity to engage in a hearty conversation, which was something Cristiano always longed for.

However, things took a turn for the better for Jose when he landed a position at a local football club called Andorinha.

Cristiano had a big heart for the game of soccer and would spend many hours outside just dribbling his ball. In fact, he seemed to be more absorbed in soccer than he was in his books. Instead of doing his homework, he would sneak out through his window with a ball to practice a few moves at the local soccer ground. There, little Ronaldo was playing for one of the greatest European teams, as he imagined the blue field lights on his face and the crowd chanting his name, "Ronaldo, Ronaldo, Ronaldo!"

As he juggled his ball up and down and weaved it between his legs, he knew he was going to be the best.

"I'm the beeeest!" the little boy shouted before his mother appeared from behind.

"Cristiano, your homework is waiting for you," his mother said, interrupting his imaginary UEFA Champions League match.

"But, Mom, when I'm done, can I go back to give the spectators a final act? You know I can't disappoint them," said Ronaldo, convinced that he was really playing in a Champions League game as he manipulated the ball with his feet as easily as putty in your hands.

Cristiano's attachment to the game went beyond love. Any chance he got, he was outside either playing a heavy game or training for one. However, his dislike for school grew in proportion with his love for soccer. Some mornings, Cristiano would ask his father if he could miss school and go along with him to Andorinha.

"Dad, I don't feel like going to school today. Can I please come to Andorinha with you?" Cristiano would ask sluggishly.

"Mhhh, you don't feel like school today? If you start with that kind of attitude now, it will become the everyday story and that isn't exactly how a prospective star behaves, young man," his father would respond.

Cristiano begged until his father relented, with a whispered reminder not to tell his mother. At Andorinha, Cristiano would have the time of his life, showing off his skill to the other kids and standing out on a team he wasn't even officially part of. In fact, the coach had been noting his football prowess and was pretty captivated by it.

"Hey kid, you have good ball control. What would you say if I said you could join my team?" asked the coach, approaching Cristiano and his father as they left the club after a long day of football.

Of course, young Cristiano agreed, and promised to be at practice every day.

Only 8 years old, his passion for the game grew and his determination was unbelievable. As the other kids arrived at practice, they would find Cristiano already in the thick of training, having arrived an hour earlier than everyone else.

He had a successful run at Andorinha and caught the attention of Nacional Desportivo, who immediately signed him.

At Nacional, Cristiano became an unstoppable footballing force. He scored so many goals and won so many awards for the team that one would think he was doing it for fun. Unfortunately, amid all the glory, he was diagnosed with a heart disorder that caused his heart to beat faster than normal. The doctors told him to take it easy on the soccer ball until he got better. After a heart surgery, Cristiano returned to normal and was ready to continue his scoring frenzy (Hendrix, 2016).

Reaching the Top

One day, the famous Sporting Lisbon visited the club, putting forth a promise to recruit whichever player scored the highest number of goals in a match. During that fiercely contested match against another local team, Cristiano performed well. However, his best friend, Albert Fantrau, played just as well. What happened next was a genuine act of friendship.

The match was nearing its end when Albert passed the ball to Cristiano instead of shooting, just so Ronaldo could take the final shot. Cristiano went straight for it, sending the ball into the net and becoming Sporting's newest member.

Albert was later asked to explain his selflessness and said that he knew Cristiano was by far a better player than he was. And just like that, Cristiano earned a position at Sporting Lisbon at the age of 16. Cristiano Ronaldo was a part of one of the biggest teams in Portugal (Hendrix, 2016). As a result of his skill and exceptional work on the pitch, his ascension to the top at Sporting Lisbon was almost instant. Starting off on the under-16 team, he bolted to the first team in less than a year. Is that awesome or what?

Now his UEFA Champions League games were no longer imaginary. He premiered against Manchester United and stood out as a star player. This prompted Man U players Patrice Evra and Rio Ferdinand to convince their coach, Sir Alex Ferguson, to sign Ronaldo and get him on board. "Sir, that boy is a phenomenal player. He would be a great addition to the team!" Patrice and Rio said after the match.

Ferguson agreed, acknowledging Ronaldo's footwork, shooting and lightning speed. "That's something we can't miss now, can we?" he agreed.

After a hefty bargain, the Sporting coach finally allowed Ferguson to sign Ronaldo in a deal that made him the most expensive teenager in football history. Cristiano played with the club for six years before eventually moving to Real Madrid in 2009.

When it comes to achieving high, Ronaldo means business. At Real Madrid, he became the first player to reach the 100-goal milestone in the Champions League. Moreover, he has scored more than 700 goals since the start of his professional career.

However, this is only the tip of the iceberg. With five Ballon d'Or awards, four Golden Shoes, three Premier League titles, and many other accolades with Manchester United and Real Madrid, Ronaldo certainly is a force to be reckoned with.

Despite his tough upbringing, Ronaldo was keen on becoming the next big thing to come out of Madeira, and he did just that. For him, it was soccer or nothing. The combined forces of poverty and sickness had nothing on his determination to be the best. Having grown up with practically nothing, he is now giving back to the world through his many philanthropic efforts. Ronaldo is living proof that hard work leads to success, and this is something we can all learn from.

Our Struggles Can Either Make or Break Us

Cristiano Ronaldo had a tough upbringing. He could have easily succumbed to this, but he did not. He pushed himself beyond limits and sought to become the star he believed he was.

Are you going through any challenges right now? How do you think you can use your challenges to achieve your dream?

What are you passionate about? What gives you a sense of accomplishment?

Write down your answers in your journal.

Consistency and Dedication

Ronaldo showed dedication to his passion—soccer—by showing up for practice earlier than the other kids on his team. How do you think you can show dedication toward your own passion?

Write down your answers in your journal.

Next up is the extraordinary story of a track and field superstar. Let's delve into chapter 4 where we'll learn all about her incredible story.

Wilma Rudolph

When the sun is shining, I can do anything; no mountain is too high, no trouble too difficult to overcome.

Behold, the girl who couldn't take a single step as a young kid, to the woman who won multiple track and field Olympic gold medals in the 1960s. With her poor health in her early years, one could have thought her incapable of achieving anything more than just lying about. Little did they know she was like a cocoon, waiting for the right time to reveal its beautiful creation.

Wilma Rudolph beat childhood disease to establish her place as the best runner in the '60s (Norwood, n.d.). Her tale is one of fate, inspiration, and the power of determination. Let us brace ourselves as we enter the life of the one and only Wilma Rudolph.

Childhood and Early life of Wilma Rudolph

Wilma Glodean Rudolph was born on June 23, 1940, in Saint Bethlehem, Tennessee. Unlike most children who spent their childhood running about and exploring the world around them, Wilma's early years were marked by struggle. At age 4, Wilma suffered bouts of double pneumonia and scarlet fever, before eventually contracting polio, a crippling disease that causes fragile bones and poor bone formation in young children.

These ailments weakened the muscles in her left leg and left her bedridden for much of her early life (Norwood, n.d.). Wilma wore a leg brace and would travel miles every week with her mother to collect medication from the doctor's office. Her appointments with the doctor were always painful reminders that she couldn't walk. In fact, her doctor once told her that she would never be able to walk again.

Those words shattered her spirit and although her family tried to cheer her up, the pain was deeply ingrained in her.

How come everyone else can walk? I think life would be so much better if I was someone else. I really wish I could be someone else, she often would think.

Sitting indoors and listening to children her age jumping rope and racing against each other was her reality. To add salt to her wounds, the neighborhood kids called her all sorts of derogatory names and made fun of her awkward gait. Although this deeply hurt her, she never lost hope. Wilma had faith that one day her legs would function normally, and she could experience all the childhood joys she had missed out on.

Sometimes, in an attempt to realize that dream, she would remove her leg brace while her parents were away so she could practice walking and running before they got back home. The pain was excruciating, but she refused to give up. Wilma was determined to walk and run like other children, and she knew that if she practiced enough, it would eventually happen. *One step at a time, Wilma. Take it one step at a time*, she would tell herself.

She took it one step at a time and because of her efforts, she regained strength in her left leg and eventually began walking normally for the first time in her life. However, her family was not aware of her progress because she had been keeping it a secret. One day when she was 12 years old, she took everyone by surprise.

It was 10:30 a.m. on a Saturday and Wilma and her mother had just returned from their weekly doctor's appointment. Her parents and siblings were gathered around the dining table for a family brunch when Wilma suddenly divulged her secret.

"Hey guys, I have something I want y'all to see," Wilma said with a smile on her face. She frantically got up from her seat and walked halfway through the room before turning and walking back to the table.

"Oh, good Lord, she can walk!" her mother rejoiced, her face blush pink with excitement.

"But... but... How? When? How did you just do that?" asked her older sister Charlene with her eyes protruding with shock.

"I've been practicing while y'all were away and I finally mastered it. I finally learned how to walk," responded Wilma.

After letting her secret out, Wilma made up for lost time by doing all the things she previously couldn't. She developed a love for challenges, competing with the boys in her neighborhood to see who was the best in sprinting and jumping. Often this was met with trash talk from her male counterparts, who doubted her abilities.

"You're just a girl! Besides, you only started walking less than a few months ago and you think you can run?" said one of the boys before a race.

"Well, I bet my bottom dollar that I'll beat you. Just wait and see." Wilma gritted her teeth before taking off.

Her speed wasn't just a bluff. Wilma outcompeted all the boys on her street and they couldn't believe how fast she was. In fact, their disbelief led them to call all the other boys in the neighborhood to race with her. However, they were simply no match for Wilma's speed.

In high school, Wilma tried to play basketball, but struggled to play it well. From the way she played so clumsily, one could see that the sport wasn't one of her strongest points (Norwood, n.d.). The coach even mocked her after she spent an entire season without a single goal or assist. However, the "go hard or go home" atmosphere helped her to chase her goals with passion.

Wilma did not have to worry about embarrassing herself again on the basketball court. After hearing about the school's newly established track and field squad, she jumped at the opportunity to join the team. From that moment, she knew she had found what she was destined to become.

Wilma proved a tough one to run against, beating all the other girls on her team. Her team had just attended a meet and there her lithe frame moved effortlessly through the lanes as she left her opponents behind and crossed the finish line.

Although everyone was shocked at her speed and agility on the track, one man in particular was extremely impressed by her stunning performance at one meet. He was the coach of Tennessee State University's track and field team.

He waited for her to get off the field and walk up to the stands before approaching her with a sweet deal.

"Wilma, I must say you are a really talented runner. I mean, I saw the way you bolted past them other kids. How do you do that?" he asked, his voice filled with conviction.

Wilma's heart beat faster. She was aware that the man talking to her had a reputation for producing Olympic-level runners. The coach adjusted his glasses and looked her in the eye. "How about you join my team at Tennessee? I believe you tick all the boxes."

With an opportunity this big, Wilma was determined to put her heart and soul into being the best that she could. She wasn't sure how she came from being bedridden to running that fast, but whatever it was, she knew that her life wouldn't be the same again. All she wanted to do was to run and see where the road would take her.

Reaching the Top

The road took her to the 1956 Olympic Games in Melbourne, Australia. At only age 16, Wilma put forth a world-class performance, clinching a bronze medal and putting America on the map (Norwood, n.d.). People who could not attend the games watched them from their home in anticipation of who she would beat next.

When she got back home to Tennessee, she became the center of attention at her school. Students praised her nonstop for her amazing performance at the Olympics.

"Yo, Wilma, let me get a quick look at your medal."

"Wow, Wilma. You did this?"

The students at her school took turns feeling the victory in her medal. Wilma was proud of her third-place medal, but each time she tried to shine it she was hit with the reality that no matter how much she tried, bronze doesn't shine.

I'm not stopping at this! The next time I get a medal, it must shine and I'm not going back on my word, she told herself.

To make this happen, she got up at 6 a.m. and hit the gym for the gold. She missed parties with her friends for the gold. She lost out on sleep for the gold. Then, at the 1960 Olympic Games in Rome, she broke three world records to get not one, but three gold medals.

During these games she set a record in the 100-meter final at 11.3 seconds. She also set a 200-meter record at 24 seconds. Her final record came as part of the U.S. 4 x 100 relay team, which won the race with a time of 44.5 seconds. (Norwood, n.d.). Wilma's exceptional speeds at the 1960 Olympic Games placed her on a pedestal as the fastest woman and the first in American history to win three gold medals in a single Olympics. For this, she was nicknamed by sport writers as "The Black Gazelle."

"Can someone please pinch me. Is this a dream or what?" she said in disbelief on the podium.

While posing for the many cameras that flashed in her face, she knew she was a champion. However, she was also reminded of the tough circumstances under which her journey began.

Less than a decade ago, I didn't know what it felt like to run, let alone to get up and walk. Now, I have run against people from all over the world and won not one but three of the gold medals they yearn for.

Wilma Rudolph didn't want this greatness to end with her. She wanted to help other children to reach their potential. This vision led her to open the Wilma Rudolph Foundation to help train potential athletes.

Rudolph's journey to the top inspired millions of people worldwide and is still touching lives to this day. To honor her bold athleticism, she was enshrined into the National Track and

Field Hall of Fame, the International Sports Hall of Fame, and the U.S. Olympic Hall of Fame in the years 1970, 1980, and 1983, respectively.

Unfortunately, after a long and painful battle against a brain tumor, she passed away in 1994 at the age of 54 in Brentwood, Tennessee. Although she has passed on, she remains a celebrated figure in American sports history.

We can all agree that Wilma Rudolph is a lot more than just a successful sports story. Hers is a story about fate and the power of determination in defying all limitations. She did the unthinkable: overcame a childhood laden with illness and misfortune to become one of the greatest women to ever happen to sports. Wilma could have easily made peace with her disability and lived with it forever. However, she challenged herself, taking off her leg brace and learning to walk. She soaked up all the difficulties brought about by her sickly childhood and used them to shape her life. Wilma's relentless drive and persistence is a reminder that nothing is impossible as long as one is determined to make it happen. Now, what is more inspiring than that?

Power of Fate

Wilma Rudolph is a testament to fate in its purest form. She is a lesson that no matter how challenging life gets or how impossible something seems, Fate is always on your side as long as you are powerful in the mind.

Think about someone you know who is going through a tough time. How can you use what you learned from this story to inspire your friend?

Write your answers in your journal.

Let us now go into the next chapter, where we will get to know how NFL quarterback Tom Brady carved out his name in NFL history.

Tom Brady

If you want to perform like a superstar, then you have to train like a superstar.

Some of you may know him from the "I'm going to Disneyland" commercials; he is the All-American quarterback and the king of the gridiron. He is none other than Tom Brady.

This football star is lauded endlessly for being the best quarterback of all time, and it is not surprising why. Because of his smart style of play, his sharp passes and his incredible aptitude for the game, he led his teams to a record-setting seven Super Bowl victories. Furthermore, he boasts impressive longevity, having played a full 23 NFL seasons including 20 with the New England Patriots and three for the Tampa Bay Buccaneers (Editors, TheFamousPeople.com, 2009). With personal achievements such as being named the NFL's most valuable player four times and the AFC's most valuable player three times, he lived the dream of any quarterback. However, behind all the success lies a story of heartache, rejection, self-doubt, and ultimately how he made it to the top. Let's go back to 1977 to see how it all started.

Childhood and Early Life of Tom Brady

On August 3, 1977, in San Mateo, California, children were playing games and the air was filled with the aroma of grilling steaks. The atmosphere in San Mateo was joyful because a legend, Thomas Edward Patrick Brady Jr., was born on this day.

Growing up in California, Tom began taking an interest in football at a young age. His older sisters Maureen, Julie, and Nancy were athletes who loved to compete. They competed over everything under the sun—shooting each other with water guns to see who got to watch TV first, or racing to the kitchen to get the last of their mom's homemade goodies. It is only logical to say that home is where Tom got his competitive drive.

For Brady, Sundays were the best days of the week because his family would take a drive to Candlestick Park to watch the San Francisco 49ers play football (Editors, TheFamousPeople.com, 2009). He had fun cheering for his favorite player, Joe Montana, and imagined himself playing on the field. On the other days of the week, if he wasn't at school, he was out playing football with his friends. Due to the lack of a backyard, he had to play on the streets and take extra care not to damage the neighbors' fences or windows.

Although Tom was incredibly talented at the passing the ball, he didn't really understand how the game of football was played. This, however, changed one day after being spotted by Tom Martinez, who was both his namesake and the man who eventually became his mentor. It was 4 p.m. and Tom was outside throwing his ball, when he suddenly heard a deep voice shouting, "Hey, sonny."

Tom looked back and saw Mr. Martinez standing across the street.

"I see you're good at football, but your skills could do with some polishing up. What do you say? I'll give you my number, then we can practice sometime?"

"Yeah, sure, that sounds amazing! I'd love that, sir."

So, whenever time allowed, the two would link up, practicing for hours and perfecting Brady's craft. After just a few sessions, he had caught on well. Tom could throw sharp passes from afar and nearby, moved at lightning speed, and maintained laser focus. This had all the other kids he played with in awe. Tom's game was so much more advanced than most of his friends' that they would run to him for advice on how they could improve their skills.

After all that practice with Martinez, the only thing that was missing was a chance to play for a real team. During his freshman year at Junipero Serra High School, the opportunity finally presented itself when he was invited to join the school's football team. Tom started as a substitute quarterback, but he worked his way up the ranks and in his junior year, he claimed his position as the starting quarterback.

Tom was versatile and his talents weren't restricted to football. His phenomenal catching abilities earned him a good reputation on the school's baseball team. The fresh, dimple-faced quarterback was such a promising prospect that by the end of his high school career, he was on almost every baseball and football scout's list.

He was invited to play professional baseball for the Montreal Expos of Major League Baseball. He also was offered a football scholarship at the University of Michigan. His heart was in football, so he chose to play for Michigan.

While he was deemed a great investment by the university, things didn't go as expected. For the first two years at the University of Michigan, he warmed the bench for prospective NFL stars like Brian Griese and Scott Driesbach. Coaches were concerned about Brady's small build, and he watched from the sidelines until he improved his physique.

Tom was generally happy, but not being given a chance to play really upset him and sometimes he thought about calling it quits and going back home to San Mateo. However, he quickly realized that running away wouldn't solve anything. He got back to his senses and continued fighting his way to the top. Tom spent his free time doing fitness training on the field and practicing how to throw impeccable passes. At times his solo training sessions would drag on late into the night. While all his schoolmates dozed off, Tom was out on the field giving his all to the sport he so dearly loved.

And, boy, did his persistence pay off. Brady finally earned the starting quarterback position on the team. He capitalized the opportunity by throwing a single-season record 350 passes and completing 214 of them.

Brady concluded his college career in 2000 being drafted by the New England Patriots in the sixth round—the 199th player taken.

Reaching the Top

Starting off that first year with the New England Patriots, he was the fourth-string quarterback. This meant that the clean-cut All-American rarely got a chance to showcase his playing abilities. Often, this was met with some unfavorable comments.

"I heard they said he's not good enough to play," he once heard someone say as he walked into the Patriots' locker room.

At times, the harsh reality of being "an option" on his team led him to question his own worth.

I probably should just keep warming the benches. I'm pathetic. I can't play. They'll probably lose with me on the playing squad, he told himself.

I give up! They are all better than I am. Why am I even here? his inner critic belittled him.

As fate would have it, events took an unexpected turn. The team's top quarterback, Drew Bledsoe, suffered an injury that left him unable to play for weeks. With this unfortunate circumstance, Brady finally got his chance in the limelight.

His impeccable performances on the field earned the Patriots their very first Super Bowl victory, in 2002. He silenced his inner critic and everyone who doubted him.

With Brady now playing full time, the team was reborn. However, this was only the beginning. Jersey #12 went on to secure another five Super Bowls with the Patriots (Editors, TheFamousPeople.com, 2009).

Brady had an incredible 20-year run with the Patriots, but as we know, all good things come to an end. His contract expired in 2019, marking a new phase in his career—a contract with the Tampa Bay Buccaneers. He continued his excellence with the Buccaneers, winning a Super Bowl while playing three years in Tampa Bay.

On February 1, 2023, Brady ended his luminous career with a record 263 career wins, 661 touchdowns, 10 Super Bowl appearances, and seven Super Bowl wins.

Tom Brady had to work hard to be recognized all his life. He knows what it feels like to not be good enough, to be sidelined, and to be seen as the weakest link on the team. However, he also knows how to rise above adversity and use his challenges to empower himself.

Success never came on a silver platter. He understood he had to get up and fight for it even when the odds were against him. It was because of his competitiveness and willpower that he fought until the end and didn't give up on his dreams.

Today, many children look up to Brady and rightfully say, "I want to be just like him." He is a perfect example of mental strength and resilience, and for this he will always have a special place in the hearts of football players and fans.

Post-Reading Reflection

Although Tom Brady was an amazing player, he had to work on his weak points by regularly practicing. This required him to know his strengths and weaknesses very well.

Are you aware of your strengths (what you are good at) and your weaknesses (what you aren't so good at)?

Sit down with your parents, coaches, or teachers and come up with a list of strengths and weaknesses.

Once you are done listing your strengths and weaknesses, plan how you will improve on your weak points.

Write everything down in your journal.

In the next chapter, we will learn about Simone Biles, who pushed herself above and beyond to become an athlete known around the world. Off we go!

Simone Biles

My aim is to always go above and beyond. That's just the act of my strong will, which I've had since I was a little child.

Introducing Simone Biles, a grand gymnast who is well known for her gravity-defying and brave acts. When it comes to nailing vault moves such as the Yurchenko double pike, she is unparalleled in the realm of gymnastics. Simone is frequently placed on par with some of the most prolific athletes of current times—Lionel Messi, Serena Williams, and Tiger Woods, to name a few.

Simone is so dominant in gymnastics that everyone who has watched her compete can unreservedly say that she is a once in a lifetime athlete. However, her journey to the top wasn't exactly easy. It was marked by difficulty and pain, particularly in her early childhood. For us to understand the road that led to Simone's success, we must go back to the late '90s and early 2000s.

Childhood and Early Life of Simone Biles

Simone Biles entered the world on March 14, 1997, in the city of Columbus, Ohio, where she spent the majority of her childhood. However, her childhood was far from perfect. Both her parents suffered from drug and alcohol addiction, which resulted in frequent fights and arguments in their home (Simone Biles, 2019).

As if this weren't enough, her father packed his things and left the family for good when Simone was only 4 years old, leaving her mother to raise four kids on her own. Unfortunately, bearing that responsibility with very little money took a serious toll on Shannon's mental health and caused her substance abuse to spike.

Shannon's indulgences meant her children didn't have enough food to eat. Despite having hungry children, Simone's mother would sometimes choose to feed a stray cat instead of them.

One day, a neighbor overheard Simone and her sibling complaining about how hungry they were and reported the situation to child services. Shannon was deemed unfit to mother her kids and in 2002, they were taken from her custody and placed in a foster home. They spent the next 12 months of their lives there.

At the foster home, they were welcomed with open arms and treated with special care. For the first time, they could eat at least three meals a day and take showers daily—a luxury their mother couldn't afford them.

Although she had now moved into a new phase of her life, Simone had a deep-rooted anger with her parents that she just couldn't shake off. She felt betrayed and like she didn't belong. Moreover, because she would see other kids being adopted by random people, she lived in constant fear that she would wake up one day and find her siblings, who were the only people left in her life, gone.

To stop that from happening, Simone would wake up at random hours of the night, doing headcounts each time to ensure her family remained intact. Luckily, she didn't have to worry about her siblings being sent off for much longer.

During their time at the foster home, their maternal grandparents, Ron and Nellie Biles caught wind of the news that their grandchildren had been placed under foster care. They set out to look for them, going from one foster home to another until they finally found them. It was just another dull summer afternoon when Ron and Nellie arrived at the foster center to claim their grandchildren. Upon arriving inside, the first thing that caught their eye was the help desk, and right there was an administrator.

"Hello ma'am, I hope you are having yourself a wonderful day. I am the grandfather of Simone, Adria, Tevin, and Ashley Biles. May I please take my grandkids home, ma'am," Ron asked the administrator with a twinkle in his eyes.

"Let me call them out and see if they know you. In the meantime, please produce your ID so that we can verify your relationship," the woman told them.

The receptionist made her way to the back to call the siblings to the foyer so that they could meet their grandparents.

"Guys, you have visitors here for you. Follow me," she said with a warm smile.

As they walked to the foyer, Simone and her siblings took turns guessing who it might be.

"I think it's mom," said Tevin

Ashley took her guess, "What if it's dad?"

Then the guesses stopped. "Hey guys, it's Granny Nellie and Grandpa Ron," Simone said, running toward them with her arms open ready for an embrace as her siblings followed behind her.

Watching as their grandparents waited to take them home was a hearty reminder that their family wasn't all that bad.

"Oh, my word, guys. Are you okay?" their grandfather said as he went in for a group hug.

"Sorry we took this long to find you. We heard that y'all were in a foster home, but we weren't sure which one," their grandmother muttered with tear-filled eyes. "But don't worry. You're coming home with us."

Unfortunately, due to their financial situation, Ron and Nellie could only afford to take care of two of them. So, they chose 6-year-old Simone and her little sister, Adria, to go stay with them in Texas. Their older siblings moved in with Ron's sister, their great aunt.

From that day forward, Simone's life changed for the better. Just a few months after moving into her grandparents' home, she went on a trip with her daycare to a gymnastics center.

Simone instantly fell in love with everything she saw. Girls were cartwheeling, some were doing splits, and others were balancing on poles to prepare for an upcoming competition. Watching the gymnasts stirred something in

Simone. The little girl saw herself up there, too, flipping and gliding through the air.

Flip, flip, and twirl. Jump, twist and flip.

She attempted to enact what she had just seen, bedazzling the many people who cheered her on as she rendered her little performance. One such person was a senior coach at the gymnasium. She was captivated by the little girl's natural talent and effortless execution of acrobatics (Simone Biles, 2019).

"What am I seeing here? This little girl is a natural!" the coach said as the crowd applauded Simone.

"You go, girl!" some of the older girls screamed in admiration.

As a result, the coach sent the Biles family a note urging them to sign her up for classes.

Good day, Mr. and Mrs. Biles,

I hope this letter finds you well. Your daughter is quite the gymnast. We all are

impressed by her moves and ask that you
get her into an academy.

This did not surprise Nellie and Ron, who had already taken note of Simone's physical prowess. Simone was always a highly active child who loved doing cartwheels and jumping from couch to couch, like popcorn popping in a pot. In fact, they sometimes feared that the girl was just too daring. Nonetheless, after sleeping on the matter, they finally thought, "Why not give it a go?" They signed her up at the Bannon Gymnastics center in Houston, Texas.

At Bannon, Simone quickly mastered every activity introduced to her. She instinctively knew that she was going to be a star.

But there was a problem. While Simone's never-ending reserves of energy allowed her to cast magic at Bannon's, at school her high level of energy was a serious cause for concern. She fidgeted constantly and struggled to concentrate on a task for long without getting distracted. This affected her academic performance.

Eventually, this unfolded as an ADHD diagnosis, which required her to be extra focused in order to overcome its effects. Being the dedicated person she was though, she became determined to overcome this problem through the power of intention. It took some practice, but eventually she could enter periods of extreme focus with conscious effort.

Simone's grandmother Nellie was focused on helping Simone set and achieve goals. At the start of every year, she took a pen and notebook and sat Simone down so they could discuss her goals and how she was going to achieve them.

In 2011, she achieved the very first of those goals when she made her national debut at the Junior National competition. The young girl outdid herself. Her flexibility and speediness earned her third place for the all-round title and first for vault.

Simone opted for homeschooling at 14 to dedicate more time to gymnastics as her career took off.

Giving up the childhood experiences that come with attending a school surely was a big change, but Simone made it worthwhile. Homeschooling allowed her to practice for six to eight hours a day, which really advanced her skill level.

Winning two all-round titles and one vault title in 2012, as well as being part of the USA Junior National team, was proof that her efforts were paying off. However, even with her awe-inspiring performances, at just 15 years old she still fell a few months short of qualifying for the 2012 Olympic team. This rejection disappointed her a bit, but she overcame it by practicing extremely hard.

Simone, I know how badly you want this to work, I know this is your dream, she constantly reminded herself. *Your time to shine is coming. All you have to do is train harder than ever before.*

Reaching the Top

As the saying goes, good things come to those who wait. Simone's time to shine came four years later, at the Rio Olympic Games in 2016 (Simone Biles, 2019). It was a golden experience for her as she delivered one of the greatest sporting acts, earning five medals. Four were gold medals—for individual wins in vault, floor exercise and all-round, as well as for the team competition.

"Put your hands together, and help us welcome the one and only Simone Biles," the commentator said as the millions in the stands and at home showed their support for the champion.

"Simone, how did you do it? What is your formula? Can we get a picture with you? OMG, Simone, we love you!" random voices shouted at the event.

It was finally real for Simone. Back in her early years, she could have never guessed she would be successful, but there she was, standing tall with pride on the podium. At only 4 feet 6 inches and 19 years old, she proved that great things do indeed come in small packages.

Today, Simone is hailed as the greatest professional gymnast of all time. She boasts a total of 32 Olympic medals and World Championships, making her the most decorated gymnast to ever walk the earth (Simone Biles, 2019). To solidify her place as a legend in the sport, Simone competes with a leotard embellished with a rhinestone goat symbol. She also has four gymnastic moves named after her.

Simone's story teaches us that rough upbringings don't determine the course of our lives. Even if things aren't looking up today, tomorrow they can change for the better. She will always be a reminder that no matter how far out of reach success may seem, we can always carve out a life of our own.

Anger Only Destroys the Vessel In Which It Is Stored

Although Simone felt a deep anger toward her parents, she had to let go of that anger for the sake of her own well-being and peace. Why do you think forgiving others is important?

Is there anyone you think you should forgive? How do you plan on doing that?

Write your answers in your journal.

That brings us cartwheeling to the end of this chapter. Don't move an inch because up next we will be joined by the famous NBA titan, Magic Johnson. Off we goooooo!

Magic Johnson

Only you have the power to make a difference. Always go for your dream, no matter what.

Meet Magic Johnson, a former point guard for the Los Angeles Lakers whose love for the game was as big as his heart. He was a luminous figure who always dared to dream big. Johnson's skills on the court led his squad to a jaw-dropping five NBA championships. He played for the Lakers for 13 years and was named the NBA Most Valuable Player three times—an achievement most players can't even imagine.

Some say that watching Steph Curry play for the Golden State Warriors is like watching Magic again. With his offensive ball handling and creative style, Magic quickly proved to be in a boat of his own. To intimately understand his road to stardom and the challenges he faced, let us go back to the mid '90s when it all began.

Childhood and Early Life of Magic Johnson

Born as Earvin Johnson Jr., "Magic" Johnson took the basketball world by storm. Most people would agree that Earvin's basketball genius came from his modest roots. His father was an autoworker during the day and a maintenance man at night, while his mother worked at a local school (Magic Johnson: African American Basketball Legend, n.d.). Despite their efforts to bring bread to the table, they often fell short of money. This sometimes forced Earvin to put aside his studies so he could work after school to help get those extra cents they needed to sustain themselves.

But money wasn't the only problem in Earvin's childhood. During his elementary years, he was diagnosed with dyslexia, a learning disorder that caused him to struggle with reading and writing. Every time he attempted to read, the words seemed to float all over the page and no matter how hard he tried, he just couldn't get it right.

Because of his disability, he often failed dismally in school, and many of his schoolmates exploited that weakness.

"Blah, blah, blah, blah, blah. Listen up, guys, Earvin is trying to read," was a common taunt.

"Just shut up, Earvin, you are making my ears sore with all that meaningless blubber. Maybe try reading alone in your room. How's that?" one of the kids said while sending a paper ball to the back of Earvin's head.

Earvin, dejected and demoralized, would just look at the other kids and continue with his work.

"Hey, man, wait up," a fellow classmate named Ted called to him one day. "Don't listen to the other kids, man. They're just jealous of you. How about we hit the courts for a game of basketball?"

"Whatever, sure man," a despondent Earvin said, shrugging his shoulders.

While things weren't so good for him in the classroom, Earvin came alive on the court. The gym was his zone, and no one could take it from him. This was clear in the way he effortlessly shot hoops and bounced about the court. He was made for the game and the game was made for him.

"Yo, slow down, Earvin. I'm running out of breath," players would say.

"Nah, dude. I'm going one more in and iiiiiiittttt's in!" he'd say as he manipulated the ball skillfully before shooting it into the hoop.

Earvin knew his predicament with reading, but he did not let that stop him from living his life. Instead, the more insults he received, the more motivated he became to work harder. Earvin dedicated a lot of time to teaching himself how to read.

However, just like everyone else, he was not without feelings. When the ridiculing got too intense for him, he would take to the courts, playing all day until sunset. Earvin eventually mastered reading in sixth grade after the school psychologist suggested extra reading classes.

Although he eventually got better at reading, his dyslexic experiences made him realize just how much he loved basketball. He was determined to hone his skill and for him, consistency was key.

Every morning, Earvin got up early to practice shooting and improve his speed at the neighborhood basketball courts. He was so consistent that a regular passerby wouldn't miss a chance to see his vibrant basketball moves at 7:30 a.m. each day. Earvin only got better with practice, and in 1973 he was named to the Everett High School basketball team. This was where he landed the nickname "Magic" after he impressed a sportswriter with his incredible ability to score, rebound, and assist with such great ease (Magic Johnson: African American Basketball Legend, n.d.).

"The boy makes it look so easy, it's magical! He should be called... Magic Johnson," the sportswriter said.

Although he was at the height of his young basketball career, the nightmares from his elementary school days were repeating themselves. This time, they came in a different form. Most students at Everett High School were white, and this often placed Magic in the center of racial prejudice. He was subjected to racial slurs and name-calling, even more so as he racked up achievements on the basketball court. However, Magic kept it cool and kept looking ahead.

Eventually, with his high school career at its end, Magic decided to go to Michigan State University and play basketball for the Spartans.

Magic's remarkable performance against Larry Bird's team in a highly charged game was unforgettable.

After having a dream of a college basketball career, Johnson could rest assured that he would be one of the top picks of the 1979 NBA draft. And that is exactly what happened. He was the first pick in the draft, selected to play for the Los Angeles Lakers (Magic Johnson: African American Basketball Legend, n.d.).

Reaching the Top

At the time, the Lakers were making big changes with a new coach and a new owner. Now, with the top basketball prospect donning purple and gold, it was game on.

In an exciting game against the San Diego Clippers early in the season, fans cheered all over the arena, the light shone brighter than ever, and the excitement was at an all-time high. The game was nearing its end and teammate Kareem Abdul-Jabbar had just pulled through with a buzzer-beater goal for the Lakers.

"Now, that's what I'm talking about! We did it! Yeah! Yeah, we did it. We did it!" Magic sang as he shuffled about in a circular motion. He couldn't hold his excitement. He was stopping at every teammate, dishing out sweaty, enthusiastic hugs.

"Yo, Kareem, we did it, man! We did it!"

"Yo hol' up, dawg. Wait a minute. We still got 81 more games to play and you are already acting like this?" Kareem said as he placed a towel around his neck and got ready to hop into the shower. "And that's 81 without the playoffs, FYI."

"He's probably gon' burn out any time now," another chuckling voice added before everyone in the room burst out in laughter.

"Nah, guys. I'm all good. I'm all good. I ain't burning out any time soon. I'm still going strong. As a matter of fact, I ain't ever burning out!" Magic responded with a smile on his face as he untied his shoes.

Magic's enthusiasm worked out in the team's favor. The Lakers won a majority of their games and claimed the NBA Championship.

Magic was certainly magical, and in 1980 he was selected to the NBA All-Star Team. He was the first player to earn that honor as a rookie since Elvin Hayes a decade earlier.

Although many people still had their doubts about Johnson, his performance during the 1980 NBA final game against the Philadelphia

76ers was enough to zip their lips. With Abdul-Jabbar on the bench recovering from an ankle injury, Magic instantly rose to the top as a hero. The 76ers were left embarrassed when Magic secured the title with an astonishing 42 points and seven assists. On top of that, he was also named the NBA Rookie of the Year. For those who ever doubted him, that game was a true testimony of just how magical Magic Johnson was.

Magic Johnson continued to draw attention with his game-changing, show-stopping style of play. Apart from leading the Los Angeles Lakers to five championships, he was also the NBA Most Valuable Player three times—in 1980, 1982, and 1987.

Unfortunately, he received a diagnosis that dictated the course of his career thereafter. In 1991, he tested positive for the human immunodeficiency virus (HIV), forcing him to make the tough decision to quit basketball before he was ready. Magic's doctors advised him to stay at home and look after his health

(Magic Johnson: African American Basketball Legend, n.d.).

Although he followed their orders for a while, in 1993, his love for basketball brought him back to the court. That year, he was selected to represent America at the 1992 Olympic Games in Barcelona, Spain, where they won a gold medal.

Magic's career will always be highly celebrated. In 2002, he was enshrined into the NBA Hall of Fame, where he now stands alongside about 175 other basketball legends such as Michael Jordan and John Stockton.

Magic Johnson is a man of rare quality. He epitomizes a positive mindset and sheer determination at its best, and is definitely someone we all can look up to. Overcoming countless challenges to become one of the greatest basketball players was far from easy, but he made it all possible. Instead of succumbing to negativity, he kept his head high and continued to chase his dreams. Magic always kept his eye on the target, practiced regularly, and gave his best in everything he did. This is why he is hailed worldwide as a basketball legend.

Post-Reading Reflection

Magic Johnson was bullied throughout his childhood for being dyslexic. The kids who bullied him thought they were cool, but bullying is never the way to go. Have you ever been bullied? If you have, how did it make you feel and how did you react to it?

Next time someone is mean to you, instead of letting them bring you down, how will you use their actions to motivate you to work harder toward achieving your goals?

Write your answers in your journal.

We have reached the very end of this chapter. Stick around with us as we go meet the best female alpine ski racer ever, Lyndsey Vonn!

Lyndsey Vonn

Chase your dreams. If you have a target that you want to accomplish, then give it your all. Eventually you'll get there.

Introducing Lyndsey Vonn, a world-famous female ski racer with an unmatched track record. Her name is synonymous with drive and determination. With 82 World Cup wins, three Olympic medals, and four all-round World Cup championships, Lyndsey Vonn is a true ski racing legend. She also has a seat at the very top as the number one ranked female skier.

Known by the monikers Kildon, Don Don and The Don, Lyndsey has shown that she has everything it takes, embodying tenacity, unrelenting perseverance, and a thirst for victory. With an illustrious career that has spanned 15 years, she has cemented her legacy in the sport as the best female skier ever.

However, her journey wasn't always blissful. Let's go back in time to see how her story began.

Childhood and Early Life of Lyndsey Vonn

The star known by many as Lyndsey Vonn was born Lyndsey Caroline Kildow on October 18, 1984, in Minnesota, where she spent most of her childhood. In his day, Lyndsey's father, Alan Kildow, was a highly competitive ski racer who had won an impressive three U.S. Junior Ski Championships before eventually retiring after a severe injury. Alan worked part-time as a skiing instructor. Lyndsey's mother, Linda Kildow, also loved sports and played several in her youth.

Therefore, it should come as no surprise that Lyndsey followed a similar path (Editors, TheFamousPeople.com, n.d.). In fact, one could say that she was born for ski racing. As young as 2 years old, Lyndsey would grab onto her father's legs and beg him to take her along to the skiing academy where he held his lessons.

"Daddy, wait, let me put on the shoes. I want to come with you," she would cry out.

"Oh, Lyndsey, but kids aren't allowed there," her father would say regretfully.

Despite her delicate age, Lyndsey was eager to learn more about skiing and eventually her dad surrendered to her pleas and let her tag along. With a look of satisfaction on her face and a sparkle in her eyes, Lyndsey would crawl into her father's backpack and await the thrill of her life. Her father snuck her into the academy, where she would sit quietly in his backpack taking mental notes of all the lessons her father had with his students.

Although his lessons seemed hard for Lyndsey to understand in the beginning, they eventually paid off. By the time she was 3 years old, Lyndsey had graduated from the "university of backpack" and was skiing on her own.

Lyndsey's love for the sport was intense, as if she were born with skis for feet! If she wasn't outside skiing with her father and grandfather, she was at Buck Hill, a local skiing and snowboarding center. There, she briefly took up lessons from ski pro Erich Sailor, a member of the U.S. National Ski Hall of Fame. At the age of 7, Lyndsey boasted an advanced set of skills that often left her peers in awe.

Her uncanny determination to become successful was so extreme that she once wrote, "I dream to get more medals than any other athlete" on a school assignment.

Lyndsey knew that if she were to realize this dream, she would have to work harder than everyone else. For most of her childhood, Lyndsey attended skiing classes at Ski Club Vail (SCV) in Colorado (Editors, TheFamousPeople.com, n.d.). But it didn't end there. She practiced on her own as well, using the nearby slopes as tools to perfect her craft.

Her relentlessness worked like magic. Among children who were at least four years older than her, she quickly stood out as the SCV's best prospect. Unfortunately, being beaten by a 10-year-old wasn't taken lightly by the other kids, who accused her of showing off and seeking the coach's favoritism.

"Boooooo, booooo. She is such a showoff!" the other kids would say. "I wonder how she even got here. She isn't even that good or maybe she's just the coach's favorite."

Because of the way she was treated, Lyndsey resorted to being a loner, and for that reason she never had many friends growing up. However, this wasn't the only adversity she faced. Her mother suffered health complications that restricted her physically and left her unable to carry out certain day-to-day tasks.

Because Lyndsey was the oldest child, she had to step up and assume a motherly role over her siblings, doing things like changing their diapers and making food, as well taking care of all the chores.

Being bullied by other children and watching her mother struggle to do much with herself pained her greatly. However, she never thought of giving up her dream. Lyndsey used her hardships as leverage to motivate herself to get where she wanted to be, working harder than ever before to shame her haters and make her mother proud.

Growing up, her ski racing role model was none other than Picabo Street. Young Lyndsey had always idolized Picabo and everything Lyndsey did was with the aim of becoming just like her. In the summer of 1995, life finally presented her with the opportunity to meet Picabo.

It was a warm and vibrant afternoon, and Lyndsey had attended a ski racing function in Colorado with her father. The first thing that appealed to her was a table where she could get Picabo's autograph. She looked at the table and there she was, her favorite pro ski racer.

"Dad, Dad. There she is. There she is, Dad! Oh, my word, I'm so excited. Can I go see her? Please, Dad?" she said as she dragged her father toward the stand.

While she waited for her turn in line, Lyndsey had her eyes fixed on Picabo the entire time. Picabo took note of this and could feel instinctively that the little girl yearned to be a ski racer. After five more kids got their autographs, Lyndsey was next in line.

"Hey, what's your name? I saw you waiting, and I just knew you were a star," Picabo said to her.

"My name is Lyndsey Kildow and I want to be just like you," Lyndsey told her.

"Well, I believe in you and I know that you can do it. How about I give you an autograph and my number, so that we can have a chat sometime," Picabo offered.

This meeting was so profound that the two continued to speak over the years, and eventually, it seemed as if Picabo had become Lyndsey's fan, too.

Reaching the Top

In 1999, Lyndsey had a breakthrough in her junior skating career. She qualified for Trofeo Topolino di sci alpino in Italy. At the competition, she and Will McDonald were hailed the first people of American descent to win a Cadet Award in the slalom category.

With her craft getting more and more polished, in 2000 Lyndsey, who had just turned 16 years old, made her World Cup debut in Park City, Utah.

Two years later, she made her Olympic debut at the 2002 Olympics in Salt Lake City, Utah. There she competed in slalom and combined racing, coming in 32nd and sixth, respectively. These Olympic games were more special because Lyndsey got to compete alongside her favorite alpine skier, Picabo Street.

Eight years later, at the 2010 Vancouver Olympic Games, she made history as the first American woman to claim an Olympic gold medal in downhill skiing. Over the course of her career, she won races in each of the five ski racing disciplines.

Lyndsey's success was a direct result of her resilience and determination. She had her fair share of falls, but with every one of them she got up, dusted herself off, and kept her eye on the target. Lyndsey had to adjust to being a loner, since all the other kids had grown jealous of her; however, she owned the situation and used it to her advantage. This she did by taking every single shortcoming as a lesson, putting her all into her passion, and making it work for her.

Lyndsey Vonn's winning spirit and love of all things skiing has filled her life and now she helps other young children find the sport. Lyndsey continues to touch lives with her story and is a reminder that with the right mindset, anything can be possible.

Jealousy

Other children were constantly jealous of Lyndsey, calling her a show-off and a rip-off. Although jealousy is a normal part of being human, when it is not controlled it can cause problems.

Here are some ways that jealousy can harm you and your relationships with others:

- **Stops us from learning new things:** When we are jealous, we are hurt that we couldn't achieve something great that someone else accomplished. In most cases, something can be learned from what other people do better than we can. So put your jealousy aside and seek to learn new things and teach others what they don't know.

- **Creates conflict:** Jealousy can strain even the healthiest of relationships, causing unnecessary resentment and anger. Sometimes, no matter how much you try to hide your jealousy, it will always reveal itself in your demeanor and this can damage your relationships with others.

- **Harms your self-image:** Jealousy goes hand in hand with a low self-image, which means how you look at yourself. It is always important to avoid being jealous so that you protect your self-image.

Is there anyone that you perhaps feel jealous of? If so, what do you think is the reason for your jealousy?

You have just learned about the negative consequences of jealousy. How do you think you can turn your jealousy into something positive? What can you do to turn it into motivation for yourself?

Write all your answers in your journal.

We have come to the end of the chapter. In the next chapter, we will rub elbows with one of the greatest hockey players ever to skate on the ice. Let's go!

Wayne Gretzky

You miss 100% of the shots you don't take.

He is the player who got the crowd rambling and bobbing up and down in anticipation of what he would do next. With an instinctive playing style that always led him directly to the puck, Canadian ice hockey legend Wayne Gretzky never ceased to amaze. In the world of ice hockey, there's no better than Wayne Gretzky—and his track record speaks for itself. In spite of his small build, Gretzky overcame his difficulties with his height and weight to become the best thing to happen to ice hockey since Gordie Howe.

While he achieved amazing successes over the course of his career in the NHL, it was his record-breaking 2,957 points, 1,963 assists and 894 goals that really sealed the deal (Wayne Gretzky Biography, n.d.). Just like many other athletes with a thirst for victory and a sincere love for their sport, Gretzky faced a lot of challenges growing up. But his unrelenting passion and determination allowed him to carve out his success story. Let us go back in time and see how the sensation that many now know and love came to be.

Childhood and Early Life of Wayne Gretzky

Wayne Gretzky came into this world on January 26, 1961, in the Canadian town of Brantford, Ontario. He was the second child of Walter and Phyllis Gretzky and enjoyed a sport-filled childhood along with his family of huge fans of hockey. The "Big Gretzky"—Wayne's father—played minor league ice hockey when he was much younger and had great hopes of becoming the next big thing, though he never did. However, this motivated him to invest in his son's hockey career.

In an attempt to make the most of his child's love for hockey, Big Gretzky built a backyard rink for little Wayne. When he wasn't busy with work, father and son spent a lot of their time immersed in the thrilling game of ice hockey.

Home wasn't the only place Wayne got to indulge in the sport. While visiting his grandfather in Canning, Ontario, Wayne played on the icy surface of the Nith River with his grandfather, who was often left shell-shocked at how talented the boy was (Wayne Gretzky Biography, n.d.).

Wayne's first chance at organized hockey came when he was just 6 years old. His incredible skill at such a young age landed him a gig playing with 10- and 11-year-old boys. Things did not go as he had wished, however. He only scored one goal in his first season with the team. This hit him hard when the season-ending award ceremony came.

"Player of the season goes to... Mario Bradley," said the coach as he handed a golden trophy to the boy.

"The award for the most assists goes to... Frank Masia," the ceremony continued.

"Last but not least, we welcome to the stage the highest scorer of the season... Sam Peters," the coach said as he handed out the final award and the crowd applauded.

Not having his name called left Wayne dejected and contemplating whether he should even come back for the next season.

"I never want to play hockey again! I'm done! Either way, I'm no good at it," Wayne said after the ceremony, throwing down his gear and kicking it out of his way.

"Wayne, stand up straight. Look at me and listen up! You want to give up on your dreams now, at this age? Wouldn't that be the highest form of betrayal to yourself?" his dad asked.

"But I'm not good and I'm the weakest link on my team. I just suck at ice hockey."

"We don't give up on our dreams, okay. Look at your favorite player, Gordie Howe. Would he have been so successful if he gave up on achieving his dreams?"

"No."

"That's the answer I'm looking for, my boy. So, what do you have to do now? Use your failures as motivation to do better next time, okay?"

"Yes, Dad."

"Now, wipe your tears away and say, 'I'm going to follow my dreams and I'm going to be the best ice hockey player ever.' "

"I, Wayne Gretzky, will follow my dreams and become the best ice hockey player ever!" he said as he went in for his father's high five.

Just like his father had advised, he took the frustration as it was and used it to motivate him to do better the next time. Every morning and evening, he would take to his backyard rink to practice for hours on end, and his efforts definitely benefited him.

As a result of Wayne's newfound attitude and passion for the sport, he became a tough nut to crack on the ice, scoring 196 goals in 76 games before turning 9 years old. The young prodigy continued on his impressive track, and by the time he was 16 years old, he had become a fan favorite. Countless fans flocked to the arenas just to see the sensation in action. At this time, he had just joined the junior A team as player number 99, a twist on his favorite player Gordie Howe's number 9.

Although he clearly was an incredible talent, his small physique was a cause for concern. Some people argued that his build meant that he wouldn't last long in the sport competing against players twice his size. Others argued it was his size that contributed to how he executed the game with such finesse. Whatever the case, he put hard work and passion into the game and trusted that everything would fall into place.

Despite his size, Wayne's coaches believed in his ability and found the perfect position for him to play safely. This decision was the birth of "Gretzky's Office," as they called his spot behind the opposition's net.

Reaching the Top

Wayne Gretzky was an irresistible sensation who everyone wanted to have on their team. By the time he was 14, he caught the attention of and was signed by teams like Toronto's Young Nats and the Sault Ste. Marie Greyhounds, winning the rookie of the year awards at both of them. In 1978, he moved to the Indianapolis Racers of the World Hockey Association in pursuit of a pro ice hockey career (Wayne Gretzky Biography, n.d.).

However, he spent just two months in Indianapolis before being purchased by the Edmonton Oilers of the WHA on a contract for a good 21 years. In 1979 the Oilers, including Gretzky, joined the NHL. Gretzky served as the captain of the team and led the Oilers to a stunning four Stanley Cup victories before joining the Los Angeles Kings before the 1988 season.

In Los Angeles, Wayne quickly established himself as a valuable and reliable member of the team. He also had a charming appeal to his fans, teammates, and opponents, which made him a people's favorite and brought a massive vibe to the team.

"Mr. Gretzky, Mr Gretzky! Can I please get your autograph?" fans asked. "You are my hero!"

In the 1989-90 season, Wayne shattered his role model Gordie Howe's long-standing record of 1,850 points in a season. Three years later, he broke Howe's 801-career goals record. These achievements gave his fans and the media more reason to celebrate him.

Gretzky later signed with the New York Rangers, the team he played with for the remainder of his career. He amassed a substantial number of awards with the Rangers before retiring in 1999.

Part of Wayne's appeal was the sportsmanship he showed throughout his career, which the NHL acknowledged with five Lady Byng awards—in 1980, 1991, 1992, 1994 and 1999. The honor is given to the NHL player who displays the best sportsmanship and highest standard of play.

The Great Wayne Gretzky hung up his famous jersey number 99, with an astounding 2,857 points, 894 goals and more assists than points scored by any other player. His dream was to be like his hero Gordie Howe—he got that and much more! In a very rare move, Gretzky was inducted into the NHL Hall of Fame in the very same year that he retired, instead of having to wait three years like everyone else.

Wayne Gretzky's success story is a true reflection of going from Zero to Hero. Scoring a single goal and the lowest number of assists for his first team was a heartbreaking reality for him. However, he took his father's advice seriously, and it worked. Listening to people doubt his abilities based on his size could have been a tremendous blow to his self-esteem, but he didn't let it affect him. By playing passionately and rising to become one of the best hockey players to ever skate onto the ice, he proved his critics wrong.

Post-Reading Reflection

Wayne Gretzky's father taught him to finish what he started and face his challenges head on. This guidance applies to all facets of life.

Every night before you go to bed, write down all the things you need to accomplish the next day. However, the catch is to list the hardest things first and the easiest ones last. Once you have listed these tasks, be sure to tackle the most difficult task first. The following is an example.

● Do my math homework
● Clean my room
● Take a bath
● Make an afternoon snack

Start making the list right now in your journal and start planning the day ahead.

Next up is a fighting champ whose kick-butt moves have taken martial arts by storm. Let's jump right into the next chapter, where her story awaits.

Amanda Nunes

It's always important to respect your opponents. This is something that life taught me. Previously, I thought that I would enter the ring and always have the upper hand. Each time I had that thought, I lost the game.

It is no secret that martial arts has been predominantly a male sport, and for a long time, there was simply no space for a female in such a sport. However, one very fierce, very brave woman dared to enter the arena, and she goes by the name of Amanda Nunes. Some people call her the Bruising Brazilian and the Lioness. Whatever she's called, she has stamped her dominance on the sport of mixed martial arts and has shown that she is here to stay. After a successful professional career that lasted for almost 15 years, Amanda is hailed the greatest female mixed martial artist of all time. The 5 foot 8, 134-pound champion has many astonishing accomplishments which only a select few gets to achieve over the course of their career. Amanda made history by becoming the first female to hold two UFC titles in different weight classes, joining the ranks of Daniel Comier and Conor McGregor. Amanda's story is filled with victories and challenges that we can certainly learn from, so let us go back to where her story began, in her native Brazil.

Childhood and Early Life of Amanda Nunes

Amanda Nunes came into the world on May 30, 1988, in Pojuca, Bahia, in Brazil as the youngest of three girls. Her childhood was not the prettiest. Just four years after her birth, Amanda's parents decided to call it quits on their marriage and live separate lives. Amanda was raised by her single mother, Ivete, alongside her two older sisters, Vanessa and Vildirene. With their father gone, life was a lot harder and they often struggled financially. To supplement the finances, her hard-working mother had to take on two jobs to support her family. Ivete worked as an administrator at a local school and as a street vendor selling candy, hot dogs, and cosmetics (Cruz, 2016).

Amanda's first love in sports was soccer, which comes as no surprise because soccer is, and has always been, a Brazilian obsession. She was intrigued by the boys who dribbled and juggled soccer balls at the neighborhood sports ground, and she really saw herself as a soccer player. Amanda went for it, playing at various soccer clubs in Pojuca and Salvador, but she didn't play for long. Her mother, who saw the sport as a distraction from her daughter's school performance, stopped Amanda from playing so she could focus on her studies.

But Amanda just couldn't focus on anything related to school. She was constantly restless and in and out of fights with the other kids at school, and this was all being observed by her teachers.

Phone call.

Teacher: Hello, is this Mrs. Nunes speaking?

Ivete: Yes, this is her. How can I help you?

Teacher: I'm calling in connection with your daughter Amanda. She has been all over the place and starting fights with the other kids, so she hasn't been able to get much work done. Please try to address this issue with her.

Ivete: Oh my, that sounds terrible. I will see what I can do about it. Thanks for taking your time to inform me.

End of call.

Now, I know my little girl can be an angry beast. I know just the right thing to help her release some of that frustration, Ivete thought.

Ivete loved martial arts. In fact, she trained in martial arts whenever her schedule allowed. One could say that for her, the knack for martial arts was more of an inherited thing since her parents and her brother Jose also took part in the sport. To handle Amanda's excessive energy, Ivete introduced her to martial arts, which became a turning point for her.

At the age of 5, Amanda began taking classes for capoeira, a native fight dance introduced to Brazil during the era of the slave trade. Amanda then moved on to karate at age 7. In the chops, kicks, and punches, Amanda discovered a deep passion for martial arts, and knew that she had found her destiny.

In most of Amanda's martial arts classes, she was the only girl, but that did not intimidate her at all. She was a brave girl who didn't mind taking down anyone who challenged her, including some of the toughest boys (Cruz, 2016).

By the time she was 16 years old, her hometown of Pujoca became too small for her ambitions, so she left for Salvador to take her career to a new level. In Salvador, she started training at the Edson Carvalho Academy.

Her sister Vanessa lived in Salvador, but a long way from the academy. Amanda gave up a comfy space at Vanessa's home, opting to stay at the dojo so she could be the first one at practice in the morning. Although other people stayed at the gym, too, Amanda was the only female. Amanda slept on the floor and by 4:30 in the morning, she would be up and ready for another day of tackling and grappling.

Her talent and fearlessness landed her the nickname "The Lioness." The academy's emblem was a picture of two lions and because all the other members were male, she took her spot as the Lioness.

Amanda was so tough that some of the boys hated to go up against her.

"I don't want to fight against her. She's a freak," they would say.

"Anyone but Amanda," the boys would confess to their coach, Edson.

Amanda breathed and lived martial arts, and it was evident in the way she hated to be away from the dojo. She hardly went out and if anyone dared to ask her when she planned to go out and have some fun, they were given an angry, "Really? Are you crazy? I want to be a star and you're telling me about going out."

Amanda wanted it, and she wanted it badly. As a result, she quickly progressed from white belt to brown. With this advancement came the realization that it was time to expand beyond her motherland, Brazil.

Reaching the Top

In 2007, she made a game-changing decision to move to New Jersey in the United States, where she would become a part of the AMA Fight Club. She trained with the club until earning her first gig as an MMA professional on March 8, 2008, in warm and sunny Miami, Florida (Cruz, 2016).

On that day, she stepped into the MMA ring, confident and vibrant as ever. The 5 foot 8 fighter danced from side to side in an attempt to intimidate her opponent, Ana Maria.

"Bring it on... ," Amanda said, clenching her fists close to her chest while the audience roared with excitement.

With the ringing of the bell, Amanda began fighting her hardest, sending a fury of punches toward her opponent. However, it was not enough to take down the tough and muscular Ana Maria. In just 35 seconds, Ana had Amanda in an armbar, and Amanda was tapping out, defeated.

She really wanted to win. In fact, she thought she was going to win, but things took a different turn. As disheartening as it was to lose so terribly in her pro debut, Amanda never backed up or took the loss personally.

She continued training and pushing herself harder than ever, and it all paid off. From the day she lost to Ana Maria onward, the Lioness became an unstoppable force, claiming victory in almost all her matches.

Amanda went on to become UFC women's featherweight champion and twice became UFC women's bantamweight champion, making history as the first woman to win a championship in two weight classes. She retired in 2023 in the number one spot in UFC women's pound-for-pound rankings (Cruz, 2016).

It is almost impossible to speak of greatness and not mention Amanda Nunes. She came from modest roots in Brazil where her mother had to work very hard to stop her kids from going to bed hungry. Then there was also growing up without her father for most of her life. Through it all, Amanda remained committed to her passion and her dream of becoming the greatest female mixed martial artist of all time. This meant making some really big sacrifices; nonetheless, she did all that she had to and eventually it all worked out.

Post-Reading Reflection

As we learned from Amanda Nunes' story, sometimes we need to make sacrifices to reach our goals. List some sacrifices you may need to make to reach your own goal.

Write them in your journal.

Coming up next is Rafael Nadal, one of the coolest people to happen to tennis. In the next chapter, we will be uncovering how he became a living legend!

Rafael Nadal

*No one wins without losing. So, I have to get
comfortable losing before winning.*

Meet the King of Clay, better known as Rafael Nadal, a tennis guru who took the tennis world by storm. Although he has for years been compared to other tennis greats like Roger Federer and Pete Sampras, what set him apart was his signature left-handed power shot and the way he moved so majestically when thwarting his opponents. With 14 French Open titles and a total of 22 Grand Slam titles, Rafael was exactly where every aspiring tennis legend would want to be (Scroll, 2022). Rafael loved a challenge, and he was not afraid to show it. He went head to head with some of the toughest opponents, only to emerge as one of the best tennis players ever. While you may all know about his gleaming victories, you may not know how he became that star player. Let us see how it all unfolded.

Childhood and Early Life of Rafael Nadal

The blazing orange sun beat as a soft breeze swept through the streets of Monacor, Spain, on June 3, 1986, marking the day Rafael Nadal was born. His parents, Sebastian and Ana Maria, and uncles Miguel and Toni Nadal all gathered around the hospital bed in celebration of his birth. Rafael gave off an aura that brightened the room. It was clear that one way or another, he was a star.

"This one is going to be a lawyer," his mother said before his uncles interjected.

"No, he's going to be a soccer player," exclaimed his uncle Miguel, who had represented Spain at the 2002 FIFA World Cup.

"Ah, ah! He is going to be the greatest tennis player ever. I bet on that," said Uncle Toni, a former junior tennis champion, as he prepared his imaginary racket to slam an imaginary ball.

Just as his uncles had prophesied, Rafael would grow to be a fanatic of both sports. By the age of 3 he was either sliding on the soccer pitch in celebration of another beautiful goal or on the tennis courts with his best bud, Ronnie, bashing tennis balls.

Rafael continued to play both sports as he entered school, but he failed to maintain a balance between sports and school, causing him to have poor grades. This was something that was met with great disapproval by his father, who was a goal-oriented entrepreneur. So, his father placed an ultimatum before him.

"You get to choose one, not both. Tennis or soccer? The choice is all yours," his concerned father told him.

The decision was tough, but young Rafael did as his father had commanded him. At the age of 12, Rafael dropped soccer and focused solely on tennis.

Uncle Toni always believed the boy was destined to become a great tennis player, but he wasn't fully aware how talented Rafael actually was. It was only after he took Rafael to the Manacor Tennis Club where Toni coached tennis that Rafael's raw talent revealed itself. What convinced him had to be the way Rafael unreservedly approached the ball (Scroll, 2022). Most of the children Toni coached were hesitant to approach the ball and waited for it to get to them before attempting to hit it. Rafael went right to the ball.

Uncle Toni taught Rafael to get out of his comfort zone at a very young age. Although the boy was right-handed, Uncle Toni pushed him to play with his left hand so that he could become more versatile.

Uncle Toni, however, wasn't the kindest of coaches. His unconventional tough love coaching style was a bitter pill to swallow for young Rafael, who often felt like his uncle was being too hard on him. For Toni, playing tennis was all about making sacrifices and being disciplined, and he tolerated nothing less than that. His approach was so hard that he didn't even congratulate Rafael or allow him to celebrate when he won a match.

Practice sessions were usually tough and unforgiving, and instead of Toni giving him a break afterward, he off-loaded a bunch of tasks for him to complete. After practice, all the other kids got to go home. However, Rafael had to remain behind, sweeping dust off the courts and picking up the balls. Uncle Toni would toss or throw balls at his nephew if he thought he was doing a bad job, making him start over. Not surprisingly, Rafael broke down one day.

"I don't want to do this anymore," Rafael shouted bitterly as he threw his racket onto the ground after a tough practice session.

His anguish did not phase his uncle, who seemed to not care about his emotional breakdown.

"You can't do this anymore? Okay, goodbye, Rafa. Go on, go home. I'll catch you there."

On the way home, Rafael had so much going through his mind. *It's all so hard. Practice. My uncle was on my back the whole time. I'm sick of it!*

However, when his rage-filled thoughts had simmered down, reality hit him hard.

"This is my dream. I want to become a tennis star. I can't quit now. I can't quit ever," he said to himself before letting out a slight roar that left passersby in doubt of his sanity. When the awkward moment had ended, he returned to his thoughts.

If I want to be the best, I'm going to have to face Toni. I know he's tough, but I need to be tougher than him.

By the time his monologue had come to its conclusion, Rafael was already approaching the doorstep of his family home. He entered the house, put his bag down, and made a post-practice snack for himself while he waited for Uncle Toni to arrive. When he finally did, it was time for the then 10-year-old to face his uncle like a man.

"Uncle Toni…"

"Uh, hmmm?"

"Sorry about what happened at the courts. I'm gonna get this right, okay?"

"Mmh, alright. You know the time and place, Rafa," Toni said before untying his shoes and wiping the beads of sweat off his forehead.

"Mallorca Tennis Club, at 3:30 p.m sharp, but I'll be there an hour earlier, sir!"

In just a few months, it became apparent that Rafael's decision to hold on to his uncle's brutal training had worked. Things were looking great for his career, and he was a widely recognized junior champion, claiming several tournaments before he turned professional.

Reaching the Top

The day was April 29, 2002, at the ATP tour and Rafael was only a few months shy of 15. A young boy with a baby face, anyone could have easily underestimated him. But Rafael was not in it for anything other than the victory. The game started off heated, and although his opponent fought hard to escape Rafael's wrath, it was nearly impossible. Finally, in that fiercely contested bout on the court, the underdog, Rafael Nadal, finally defeated his opponent, Ramon Delgado.

"He is so good, but he is so young... ," viewers commented.

"But he's such a baby. How?" the spectators said in disbelief at what had happened.

With that match, Rafael became just the ninth teenager to win an ATP match before age 16. That quickly proved to be just the tip of the iceberg. In just two years, he had become the youngest male since Boris Becker to make it to a Wimbledon quarterfinal.

In 2004, Raphael was welcomed onto the Spanish national team, where he played a fundamental role in helping bring down the United States in the Davis Cup final. There he defeated Andy Roddick, who was at the time the world number two, and claimed his title as the youngest player to win a singles Davis Cup match for a winning team. The young man was only 18 years and six months old.

Everything looked great for him as he went on to amass a collection of medals and titles. This collection includes an astounding 22 Grand Slam men's singles titles and 92 ATP singles titles, 36 of which were Masters titles. His dominance on the clay court—63 wins—made him the certified King of Clay (Scroll, 2022). He also won two Olympic gold medals.

Rafael Nadal had to endure his uncle's tough training sessions in his quest to become the star he had always dreamed of becoming. He took the hard lessons for what they were, deciding to work harder and follow his uncle's advice.

He established himself as a star and a legend to be reckoned with. His story is one of grit, hope, determination, and the power people have to turn dreams into reality.

Post-Reading Reflection

Rafael Nadal had his own share of challenges to overcome, particularly his uncle Toni's tough training. Ask your mom, dad, or grandparents if they have ever been in a challenging situation and if they think the challenge helped them in any way. Write your findings in your journal so you can think more about it.

You have read all about Rafael and his journey to stardom. Now, we set off to the speedy racetracks of F1 to meet our final athlete!

Lewis Hamilton

You can knock me down, but I get up twice as strong.

In the high-octane world of Formula 1, where the roar of engines and the scent of burning rubber signify the battleground of speed, one name has risen above the rest: Lewis Hamilton. A maestro behind the wheel, Hamilton has carved his name into the history books of racing. With a record equaling seven World Championship titles, this British racing prodigy has not just raced; he has redefined what it means to be a champion.

Childhood and Early Life of Lewis Hamilton

On the brisk winter day of January 7, 1985, in the humble town of Stevenage, England, a future legend was born. Lewis Carl Davidson Hamilton entered the world, bringing with him a spark that would one day ignite the tracks of Formula 1 with unparalleled brilliance. His parents, Carmen and Anthony Hamilton, named him after the American sprinter Carl Lewis, perhaps an early nod to the speed that would come to define their son's life.

From the outset, Lewis's family life was a patchwork of challenges and love. His parents separated when he was just two, and he would spend his early years shuffling between their homes. It was in these formative years, amid the backdrop of his mother's nurturing and his father's determination, that Lewis's racing spirit began to take shape.

The gift of a radio-controlled car from his father when he was 6 years old was more than a toy; it was a gateway to his love for racing. Lewis would maneuver it with such skill that it seemed to dance under his command. His father, recognizing a hint of the raw talent that lay within Lewis, made a pivotal decision. Anthony Hamilton supported his son's dream by giving him a go-kart for Christmas at the age of eight, despite it being out of his budget.

The very next day, Lewis joined the local Rye House Kart Circuit, who didn't just witness Lewis's early turns, it was where we started to really hone his skills. Under the watchful eye of his father, who assumed the roles of mentor, manager, and chief mechanic, Lewis honed his craft. Anthony's unwavering commitment meant long hours and multiple jobs to fund the racing endeavors, but the sight of Lewis on the podium, trophy in hand, made every sacrifice worthwhile.

Lewis's talent was undeniable, but it was his relentless work ethic, instilled by his father's mantra, "Always more work to do," that set him apart. He would arrive at the track when the morning dew was still fresh, and wouldn't leave until the sun dipped below the horizon. Each race was more than a competition; it was a lesson in resilience, a test of character, and a chance to inch closer to his dream.

As he grew, so did his collection of trophies, each one a testament to his increasing skill and unrelenting drive. His peers would often remark, not just on his natural ability, but on his meticulous attention to detail and the methodical way he would dissect each race, learning from every turn, every victory, and every defeat.

By the age of ten, Lewis's reputation had become significant in his hometown. He wasn't just a kid with a go-kart; he was a young prodigy with his eyes firmly set on the pinnacle of racing - Formula 1. And with the support of his family, the guidance of his father, and a heart full of dreams, Lewis Hamilton was accelerating towards greatness, one race at a time.

Reaching the Top

As the young Lewis Hamilton's prowess on the karting circuits grew, so did the whispers of his potential to reach the top of motorsport. His father's sacrifices and his own relentless pursuit of perfection were about to set the stage for a seismic shift in the world of racing.

At the age of thirteen, Lewis's life took a pivotal turn. In a moment that seemed to be pulled from a storybook, he approached Ron Dennis, the boss of the McLaren Formula 1 team, at an awards ceremony. With the poise of a seasoned negotiator and the innocence of a child, Lewis introduced himself and declared, "One day I want to be racing your cars." Ron, impressed by the young man's confidence, scribbled a note in his autograph book: "Phone me in nine years, we'll sort something out then."

But destiny, it seems, had a faster timeline in mind. In less than three years, Lewis joined the McLaren Driver Development Support program, becoming the youngest driver to earn a contract.

The path to the top was not a straight line though; it was a circuit with its own set of twists and turns. Lewis ascended through the ranks, from karting to cars, facing new challenges at every level. In the junior formulas, he showcased a blend of raw speed and tactical intelligence, a combination that saw him outpace and outsmart his rivals. His rise through the ranks was meteoric, capturing titles in the Formula Renault UK series, the Euro F3 series, and finally, the GP2 series, which is widely regarded as the final stepping stone to Formula 1.

In 2007, Lewis's dream crystallized into reality. He was announced as a McLaren F1 driver, taking his place on the grid among the very best in the world. His debut season was a revelation; he stood on the podium in his first nine races, a record for a rookie, and narrowly missed the World Championship by a single point.

The following year, Lewis's relentless pursuit of excellence paid off. He clinched the World Championship in a dramatic fashion, overtaking on the last corner of the last lap in the last race of the season. It was a victory that echoed around the world, a testament to his skill, his courage, and his unwavering determination.

Lewis Hamilton had reached the top, but he was far from done. With each season, he continued to evolve, to adapt, and to overcome. His driving style, aggressive yet calculated, his strategic mind always two steps ahead of the competition, and his physical and mental stamina made him not just a driver to be reckoned with, but a legend in the making.

Over the years, he has not just maintained his position at the pinnacle of the sport but has continued to push the boundaries of what is possible. His driving evolved, as did his approach to sport and life. He also became a voice for change, advocating for diversity and environmental sustainability, using his platform to drive forward not just cars, but conversations that matter.

As he continues to compete, breaking records and setting new standards, Lewis Hamilton's legacy is not solely defined by the number of championships or race wins. It is encapsulated in the way he has inspired a generation to dream, to strive, and to never relent in the pursuit of greatness. His story is a testament to the power of passion, the importance of perseverance, and the beauty of believing in oneself.

Post-Reading Reflection

Lewis Hamilton's story is not just one of personal triumph, but also one of adaptation and evolution. His career shows us that success often requires change, sometimes even a change within ourselves. Think about a hobby, skill, or subject you once found difficult or uninteresting. Talk to someone you admire about how they've improved in something they love.

What did they do differently? How did it change the outcome? Write down their story and strategies in your journal. Reflect on how you can apply these strategies to embrace change and grow in your own pursuits.

Conclusion

Now that we have come to the end of the book, you are all set to become the young achiever you were meant to be. The morals of these stories apply to many aspects of your life. They are just what you need to sustain your journey to success.

From the story of Babe Ruth, you learned that sometimes, all you need to do is change your behavior in order to become successful. With the help of Brother Matthias, Babe reformed himself from his old ways and became a great baseball player.

How about Maria Sharapova, who overcame poverty, loneliness, and bullying to become a tennis legend? Maria gave herself messages of affirmation every morning to ensure she maintained a positive outlook on her rather painful life. She worked hard, trained every day, and never gave up on what she loved.

Then there was Wilma Rudolph, who went from being bedridden for the first 12 years of her life to being the fastest woman in the world. Despite being told by her doctor that she may never be able to walk, she believed in herself. Wilma knew that she would walk one day. She was confident in her abilities and eventually she got up one day to not only walk, but run, and she took the track and field world by surprise.

Let us not forget the remarkable story of Tom Brady, who endured being a bench warmer during the earliest phases of his career. He had to work his way up from invisibility to stardom, and remain positive while he did it. The thought of giving up constantly visited his mind, but because he knew exactly what he wanted to achieve, he never gave into it.

In situations like these, most people would have given up. But sometimes all one really needs to do is cry if they are hurt, punch a punching bag if they are angry, and come back out to do better than the last time. You just need to remind yourself of your goals and purpose. We all go through unique problems, but problems are not to be seen as limitations.

Instead, they should be viewed as stepping stones to greatness, so don't give up on what you love.

By adopting the resilience, grit, and perseverance of these athletes, the life of your dreams is within reach.

The power to become anything you want is right in your hands. You have the ability to make all sorts of things happen for yourself. By working hard and believing in yourself, you can become the best athlete on your team, a straight-A student, or even the best artist you can be! You just have to unleash the power in you.

Don't keep this knowledge to yourself though. Your friends and family may love to hear a word or two of advice, so go on, spread the knowledge and help others overcome their struggles and become their best selves.

Leave Your Feedback on Amazon

Please think about leaving some feedback via a review on Amazon. It may only take a moment, but it really does mean the world for small authors like myself :)

Even if you did not enjoy this title, please let me know the reason(s) in your review so that I may improve this title and serve you better.

From the Author

As a retired school teacher, my mission with this series is to create premium educational content for children that will help them be strong in the body, mind, and spirit via important life lessons and skills.

Without you, however, this would not be possible, so I sincerely thank you for your purchase and for supporting my life's mission.

Don't forget your free gifts!

(My way of saying thank you for your support)

Simply visit **haydenfoxmedia.com** to receive the following:

- 10 Powerful Dinner Conversations To Create Amazing Kids

- 10 Magical Affirmations To Help Kids Become Unstoppable in Life

(you can also scan this QR code)

More titles you're sure to love!

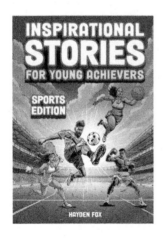

Printed in Great Britain
by Amazon